The End-Times Warrior

A 40-Day Devotional

PATRICIA A. DANIEL

The End-Times Warrior
A 40-Day Devotional
2025 © by Patricia A. Daniel
All rights reserved. Published 2025.

BIBLE SCRIPTURES

This book was created with the assistance of the AI for formatting and content editing purposes. The final content has been fully reviewed and edited by the author, who is the sole owner of the copyright for the book's content.

Published in the United States of America by

 SPIRIT MEDIA

Spirit Media Inc
https://spiritmedia.us

Spirit Media and our logos are trademarks of
Spirit Media Inc
8045 Arco Corporate Drive STE 130
Raleigh, NC 27617
1 (888) 800-3744

Religion & Spirituality | Christian Books & Bibles | Spiritual Growth
Paperback ISBN: 979-8-89307-153-5
eBook ISBN: 979-8-89307-154-2
PDF ISBN: 979-8-89307-155-9

Cover Inspiration: Isaiah 66:15-16

Foreword

Dear Reader,

When I was growing up as a child of military parents, I witnessed firsthand the discipline, order, and unwavering commitment displayed by those who served in our armed forces. Little did I know that God would use this experience to shape my understanding of what it means to serve under the command of our Lord Jesus Christ. It was not too long ago that I penned a poem called *Marching Orders* about being prepared to serve faithfully in the end-times. I never imagined that God would eventually use this poem to be the inspiration behind the devotional you will be reading.

God is raising up His End-Times Warriors—men and women who will dare to believe, trust, and obey Him at ANY COST. These warriors are dead to self, but fully alive to God and His divine purpose. They are unstoppable, unlimited, fearless, and empowered as they surrender completely to the Holy Spirit, operating in His unlimited anointing and power. The End-Times Warrior remains loyal to Christ and His Kingdom regardless of personal cost, trusting in God's sovereignty and standing ready to obey, even unto death. I believe the body of Christ may not fully comprehend the season that lies ahead—a time of persecution that may call some to martyrdom. Yet there are those whom God is preparing even now, and He will accomplish His purposes through them.

For many of us, recent years have served as a difficult training ground—a season of preparation with many opportunities

III

to die to fear, self-reliance, and personal agendas. Through these "death experiences," we've discovered the freedom that comes when we depend on Christ alone. We can now understand the urgency of our mission, and the required depth of our loyalty and obedience to trust Him to fulfill whatever He calls us to do, no matter what.

This 40-day devotional by no means captures the full breadth of all God is doing in us and for us in these end-times, but it can serve as a roadmap to help us be ready for His return. In this devotional, we dive deep into the biblical truths about our Commander, our identity in Him, His sovereign training of His warriors, and the warrior's transformed mindset. Each day contains a biblical truth, a reflection on that truth, ideas for how to apply it, a prayer, and a closing affirmation of faith. A page for note taking is also provided.

May this devotional serve as our trumpet call, awakening us to new levels of faith, commitment, and obedience. May the Lord make us fearlessly ready to follow His every command, trusting completely in His sovereignty and unfailing love.

We have received our marching orders and now is the time to put on the man of war, our Lord Jesus Christ, and rest in the fullness of His grace.

Gracefully,

Patricia A. Daniel

Dedication

To Azaiah, my grandson and favorite warrior

and

To the great cloud of witnesses, who have run before us and inspired me with their perseverance and faith, and who although unseen, yet testify to what is possible when we fix our eyes on Jesus.

May their steadfast example inspire all who read these pages to lay aside every distraction to embrace the race set before them with endurance and hope, and to look always to the Author and Perfecter of our faith.

From their testimonies, we find purpose, courage and strength and have witnessed the grace of God in their lives. We courageously join their ranks, as witnessing warriors for Christ into eternity.

Hebrews 12:1-3 (NKJV)

Table of Contents

"The LORD is a man of war; The LORD is His name."
Exodus 15:3 (NKJV)

TODAY'S AFFIRMATIONS

My Commander is the Lord of hosts, and under His leadership, I cannot be defeated.

I move when He says move, I stand when He says stand, and I follow where He leads, confident in His perfect strategy for victory.

I am an elite warrior under the command of the LORD, a man of war. My position is offensive, unstoppable, and victorious.

I am free from fear, fully surrendered, and ready to fulfill my divine assignment for such a time as this.

THE LORD, OUR COMMANDER

DAY 1: We Serve A Man Of War

Every warrior must first understand who their commander is. Our Commander is none other than the LORD Himself—a man of war. This powerful declaration from Exodus reveals a facet of God's nature that we often overlook. He is not merely a peaceful, passive deity, but a strategic, powerful warrior who engages in battle against the forces of darkness.

This isn't merely a comforting thought; it's a declaration of the position from which we fight. When Moses and the Israelites stood at the shores of the Red Sea, having witnessed the mighty hand of God defeat Pharaoh's army, they didn't sing praises to their own strength or strategy. They recognized the true source of their victory: the Lord, the man of war.

As end-times warriors, we don't fight under human leadership or worldly authority. Our commander is the Lord of hosts, the King of kings, who has never lost a battle and never will. His position is offensive, unstoppable, and victorious—and as His soldiers, we operate from that same position.

Under His command, our position becomes clear: we are offensive, not merely defensive; unstoppable, not easily deterred; and victorious, not defeated. Like elite military forces—Navy SEALs, Delta Force, and Army Rangers—we have been specifically chosen, rigorously trained, and uniquely prepared for spiritual warfare. We are not ordinary soldiers but special-ly equipped warriors in an elite class, entrusted with missions that require extraordinary courage, unwavering commitment, and absolute surrender.

The character and mindset of an end-times warrior reflects this elite calling. Free from debilitating fear, we have entrust-ed our very lives to our Commander and surrendered every-thing to His authority. We recognize that we've been chosen "for such a time as this"—to fulfill a divine assignment in this critical moment of history. This is an urgent rescue mission, and the time for action is now. Like our Commander who laid down His life, we too are ready to sacrifice everything for the cause of Christ.

True warriors serve with humility, considering themselves "the least of all," following orders without question or excuse. They remain undistracted by personal expectations, emotions, envy, or entitlement. With no hidden motives or agendas, they serve with pure hearts, knowing they are divinely protected and need not defend themselves. Though they serve as kings and queens under the King of Kings, they bear only the name of Jesus, preferring to remain anonymous—"unknown sol-diers" in His great army.

In God's kingdom, the greatest warriors view themselves as "zeros amongst zeros," serving the only true Hero who is worthy of all glory, honor, and praise. This paradoxical posi-tion—being both royal and humble, both powerful and sub-missive—defines the warrior's identity in God's kingdom.

THE LORD, OUR COMMANDER

Reflection

Take inventory of your spiritual readiness as a warrior in God's army. Where do you still struggle with fear? What have you not yet fully surrendered to your Commander? Identify one area where personal expectations, emotions, or ambitions may distract you from your mission.

Consider writing a personal declaration of surrender, explicitly handing over to God those areas you've been reluctant to release. Recognize the honor of being chosen for "such a time as this" and accept your assignment with renewed determination.

Examine where you've placed your trust. Have you been relying on your own strength, wisdom, or resources? Have you sought guidance from worldly sources rather than your divine Commander? Make a conscious decision to realign yourself under His command and embrace your identity as an elite warrior in God's army, recommitting yourself to serve without question or excuse.

Action

When facing challenges today, pause and visualize yourself receiving orders directly from the Lord. Before making decisions, ask: "What would my Commander have me do in this situation?" Remember that you don't fight alone or under your own authority, but under the banner of the Lord of hosts.

Prayer

LORD, my Commander, I acknowledge You today as the man of war who stands at the head of Your army. Forgive me for the times I've attempted to fight battles in my own strength or under my own authority. I submit myself fully to Your command. Give me ears to hear Your battle instructions and courage to follow where You lead. Help me to recognize Your voice above all others and to move when and how You direct. LORD, my Commander, I stand in awe that You—You have chosen me to serve in Your elite forces. Forgive me for the times I've forgotten who You are and who I am in You. Remove all fear from my heart and help me surrender everything to Your command. I acknowledge that You have chosen me for this specific time and assignment in history. Make me ready to serve without question or excuse, free from distractions and hidden motives. Strip away my need for recognition and self-protection. I am Your servant-warrior, bearing only Your name, seeking only Your glory. Though I am but a zero among zeros, I serve the Hero who is worthy of all praise. Use me as You will in Your unstoppable, victorious campaign. In the mighty name of Jesus, Amen.

Journal

_____

_____

_____

_____

_____

_____

_____

_____

_____

_____

_____

_____

_____

_____

_____

_____

_____

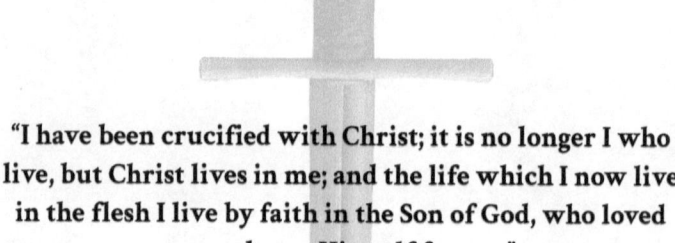

"I have been crucified with Christ; it is no longer I who live, but Christ lives in me; and the life which I now live in the flesh I live by faith in the Son of God, who loved me and gave Himself for me."
Galatians 2:20 (NKJV)

TODAY'S AFFIRMATIONS

I am crucified with Christ; it is no longer I who live, but Christ who lives in me.

In surrender, I find strength; in yielding, I find victory.

I am dead to self but alive to God, and through Him, I am unstoppable.

THE WARRIOR'S IDENTITY IN CHRIST

DAY 2: The Surrendered Warrior

The paradox of spiritual warfare is that our greatest strength comes through complete surrender. The end-times warrior understands that victory isn't found in asserting ourselves but in yielding fully to Christ. When Paul declared, "I have been crucified with Christ," he was describing the warrior's posture—dead to self-interest, personal ambition, and worldly attachment.

This crucified life is the secret weapon of the end-times warrior. When you have surrendered all—your plans, possessions, reputation, comfort, and security—you become unstoppable. The enemy has nothing to threaten you with, no leverage to use against you. Your life is hidden with Christ in God, and from this place of death to self, true power emerges.

Consider how Jesus modeled this surrendered warrior posture. Though He was God, He did not consider equality with God something to be grasped but made Himself nothing, taking the form of a servant. His surrender led to the cross, which appeared to be defeat but was actually the greatest victory in history. As you follow His pattern of surrender, you too will discover power in weakness and victory through yielding.

Reflection

Take inventory of what you're still holding back from God. What possessions, relationships, ambitions, or comforts have you been unwilling to surrender? Write these down, then offer them to God as a warrior laying down his personal weapons to take up kingdom weapons instead.

Action

Practice servanthood today as an expression of your surrender. Look for opportunities to serve others without recognition or reward. Embrace tasks that your ego resists as beneath you. Remember that in God's kingdom, the way up is down.

Prayer

Lord Jesus, I marvel at Your example of complete surrender. Today, I choose to be crucified with You—to die to my self-interest, ambition, and worldly attachments. I surrender everything that I have been holding back: my future, my reputation, my comfort, my security, my plans. I am no longer my own; I belong fully to You. Live Your life through me. Fight Your battles through me. Accomplish Your purposes through me. May it no longer be I who live, but Christ who lives in me. In Your name, Amen.

Journal

_____

_____

_____

_____

_____

_____

_____

_____

_____

_____

_____

_____

_____

_____

_____

_____

_____

_____

**"Put on the whole armor of God, that you may be
able to stand against the wiles of the devil."**
Ephesians 6:11 (NKJV)

TODAY'S AFFIRMATIONS

I am fully equipped for spiritual battle with God's own armor.

I stand protected against every scheme of the enemy, ready to
advance the kingdom with divine weapons that are mighty for
pulling down strongholds.

THE WARRIOR'S IDENTITY IN CHRIST

DAY 3: The Equipped Warrior

No military commander would send soldiers into battle without proper equipment, and our Commander is no exception. As an end-times warrior, you have been issued divine armor designed specifically for the spiritual battles you face. This isn't metaphorical equipment—it's real spiritual protection and weaponry that determines your effectiveness in warfare.

The belt of truth secures everything else in place. In an era of deception and shifting ideologies, you stand firmly grounded in God's unchanging truth. The breastplate of righteousness—Christ's righteousness imputed to you—protects your heart from condemnation and accusation. Your feet are prepared with the gospel of peace, providing stable footing on any terrain. The shield of faith extinguishes even the most fiery attacks from the enemy. The helmet of salvation guards your mind against doubt and fear. And the sword of the Spirit—God's Word—is your offensive weapon, cutting through deception and darkness.

This divine armor isn't something you create or earn; it's issued to you by your Commander. Your responsibility is to consciously put it on daily, recognizing your complete dependence on God's provision rather than your own strength or strategy.

Reflection

Identify which piece of armor you've been neglecting. If it's the belt of truth, commit to deeper study of God's Word. If it's the shield of faith, practice speaking faith declarations over areas of doubt. If it's the sword of the Spirit, memorize scripture verses relevant to your current battles.

Action

Begin each morning this week with a deliberate practice of "putting on" the full armor of God. Visualize each piece as you pray through Eph. 6:14-17, acknowledging your need for divine protection and equipping.

Prayer

Heavenly Father, thank You for providing the spiritual armor I need for battle. Today, I deliberately put on the belt of truth—anchoring myself in Your unchanging Word amidst a world of lies. I put on the breastplate of righteousness—not my own righteousness but Christ's, protecting my heart from accusation. I prepare my feet with the gospel of peace—ready to stand firm and advance Your kingdom. I take up the shield of faith—trusting You completely regardless of circumstances. I put on the helmet of salvation—guarding my mind against doubt and fear. And I wield the sword of the Spirit—Your powerful Word that cuts through deception. Equipped by You, I stand ready for whatever this day brings. In Jesus' name, Amen.

_____

_____

_____

_____

_____

_____

_____

_____

_____

_____

_____

_____

_____

_____

_____

_____

_____

_____

_____

_____

_____

_____

_____

_____

_____

_____

_____

_____

_____

_____

_____

_____

_____

_____

_____

_____

_____

"Behold, I give you the authority to trample on serpents and scorpions, and over all the power of the enemy, and nothing shall by any means hurt you."
Luke 10:19 (NKJV)

TODAY'S AFFIRMATIONS

I have all power and authority given to me by Jesus Christ.

I exercise this authority over every work of darkness.

The enemy must flee at my command because I speak not in my own name but in the name of Jesus, before whom every knee shall bow.

THE WARRIOR'S IDENTITY IN CHRIST

DAY 4: The Authorized Warrior

Authority is different from power. Power is the ability to do something; authority is the right to exercise that power. As an end-times warrior, you've been granted both—divine power and the authority to use it against the enemy. This isn't authority you've earned or deserved; it's delegated authority from Jesus Christ Himself.

When Jesus spoke these words to His disciples, He was commissioning them with the same authority He operated in—authority that made demons tremble and disease flee. This authority wasn't limited to the original disciples. It extends to all believers who recognize their position in Christ. As joint-heirs with Him, seated in heavenly places, you operate with delegated authority in His name.

The enemy understands authority. When you speak and act with the conscious awareness that you represent your Commander, the forces of darkness must respond not to your personal power but to the authority you represent. This is why praying, speaking, and acting "in Jesus' name" isn't a religious formula—it's a declaration of the authority by which you operate.

Reflection

Identify areas where you've been passive, allowing the enemy ground he has no right to occupy. Write these down, then speak words of authority, reclaiming that territory for the kingdom of God.

Action

Practice exercising your spiritual authority today. When facing temptation, speak directly to it: "In the name of Jesus, I command you to leave." When encountering negative thoughts or emotions, use your authority: "I take this thought captive to the obedience of Christ." When interceding for others, pray with authority rather than uncertainty.

Prayer

Lord Jesus, thank You for delegating Your authority to me as Your warrior. I acknowledge that this authority comes from You alone—not from my own righteousness, wisdom, or strength. Today, I consciously take up the authority You've given me to trample on serpents and scorpions and over all the power of the enemy. I speak to mountains of opposition in my life and command them to move in Your name. I bind the work of the enemy and loose Your purposes in my life, family, and sphere of influence. Thank You that nothing shall by any means hurt me as I operate under Your authority. In Your mighty name, Amen.

Journal

_____

_____

_____

_____

_____

_____

_____

_____

_____

_____

_____

_____

_____

_____

_____

_____

_____

**"For God has not given us a spirit of fear, but of power
and of love and of a sound mind."**
2 Timothy 1:7 (NKJV)

TODAY'S AFFIRMATIONS

I am free from fear because my life is fully entrusted to my Commander.

I operate in a spirit of power, love, and a sound mind.

No weapon formed against me shall prosper, for the Lord Himself is my shield and defender.

THE WARRIOR'S IDENTITY IN CHRIST

DAY 5: The Fearless Warrior

Fear is the first weapon the enemy deploys against a warrior, because he knows that a frightened soldier cannot fight effectively. But as an end-times warrior, you have been liberated from fear's paralyzing grip. The spirit that operates in you isn't one of timidity or cowardice—it's a spirit of power, love, and self-discipline.

This fearlessness isn't born of naive optimism or false bravado. It emerges from a profound understanding that your life is fully entrusted to your Commander. When you've surrendered everything—your safety, your comfort, your reputation, even your very life—what remains to fear? The warrior who has already died to self cannot be threatened with death.

You stand in a long line of fearless warriors who understand this truth. Stephen faced stoning with a face like an angel. Paul and Silas sang hymns in prison at midnight. The martyrs throughout church history went to their deaths with songs of praise on their lips. This is your heritage as an end-times warrior—not cowering in fear, but standing in bold confidence, knowing that nothing can separate you from the love of Christ.

Reflection

Identify specific fears that have held you back from fully embracing your role as an end-times warrior. Name them explicitly, then surrender each one to your Commander.

Action

Practice fearlessness in small ways today: Speak truth when it would be easier to remain silent. Take a step of faith when you'd rather play it safe. Reach out to someone when rejection seems possible. Each small victory over fear strengthens you for the greater battles ahead.

Prayer

Lord Jesus, I confess that I have allowed fear to limit my effectiveness as Your warrior. Today, I renounce the spirit of fear and embrace the spirit of power, love, and a sound mind that You have given me. I entrust my life fully into Your hands—my safety, my provision, my future, and my reputation. What can man do to me when my life is hidden with Christ in God? Strengthen me to stand fearlessly against every scheme of the enemy, knowing that You have already secured the ultimate victory. In Your mighty name, Amen.

Journal

_____

_____

_____

_____

_____

_____

_____

_____

_____

_____

_____

_____

_____

_____

_____

_____

_____

_____

_____

_____

_____

_____

_____

_____

_____

_____

_____

_____

_____

_____

_____

_____

_____

_____

_____

_____

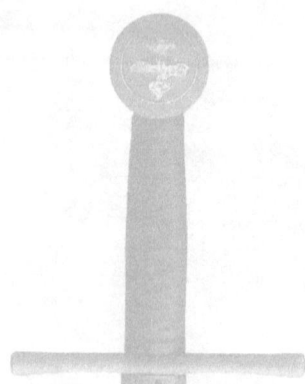

"But thanks be to God, who gives us the victory through
our Lord Jesus Christ."
1 Corinthians 15:57 (NKJV)

TODAY'S AFFIRMATIONS

I fight from a place of victory, not for victory.

The battle belongs to the Lord, and He has already triumphed.

Through Christ, I am more than a conqueror, and nothing can
separate me from His love or defeat His purposes in my life.

THE WARRIOR'S IDENTITY IN CHRIST

DAY 6: The Victorious Warrior

The end-times warrior fights from a fundamentally different position than the world understands. While others struggle desperately for victory, we fight from victory already secured. Our Commander has already won the decisive battle at Calvary, and His resurrection is the guarantee of our triumph.

This doesn't mean we won't face battles—we most certainly will. But it completely transforms how we approach them. We don't fight with the desperate energy of those uncertain about the outcome. We don't battle with the fear of defeat clouding our vision. Instead, we engage with confidence, knowing that our Commander has gone before us, securing victory before we ever enter the field.

Jesus said, "Be of good cheer, I have overcome the world" (John 16:33). This is the battle cry of the end-times warrior. Even as darkness seems to intensify and opposition grows stronger, we stand in unshakable confidence, knowing that victory isn't something we're striving to achieve—it's something we're stepping into by faith.

Reflection

Think of a situation in your life where you've been fighting with uncertainty, as if the outcome were in question. Reframe your approach to this battle, consciously choosing to fight from victory rather than for victory. This shift in perspective will change your strategy and confidence.

Action

Create a "victory declaration" based on scriptural promises that you can speak over current challenges. Begin each declaration with "Thanks be to God who gives us the victory through our Lord Jesus Christ" and then specifically name the area where you're claiming victory.

Prayer

Victorious Lord, I praise You today for the victory You've already secured at Calvary. Thank You that I don't have to strive for a victory that's uncertain—I can rest in a victory that's guaranteed. As I face battles in these end times, help me to keep my eyes fixed on You, the author and finisher of my faith, who for the joy set before You endured the cross. Thank You that the outcome is never in question. The enemy has been defeated, death has lost its sting, and Your kingdom will prevail. I choose to live and fight today from this position of victory, advancing Your kingdom with confidence and joy. In the name of Jesus, my victorious King, Amen.

Journal

_____

_____

_____

_____

_____

_____

_____

_____

_____

_____

_____

_____

_____

_____

_____

_____

_____

_____

> **"Being confident of this very thing, that He who has begun a good work in you will complete it until the day of Jesus Christ."**
> Philippians 1:6 (NKJV)

TODAY'S AFFIRMATIONS

I am in elite spiritual training under the Lord's command.

Every challenge strengthens me, every test refines me, and every experience prepares me.

I am being equipped for an extraordinary assignment in these end-times, and I embrace my training with courage and gratitude.

THE WARRIOR'S
SPECIAL TRAINING

DAY 7: The Sovereign Training Of His Warriors

Just as elite military units undergo specialized training to prepare them for extraordinary missions, you too have been in God's special operations training program. The challenges, trials, and tests you've endured weren't random hardships—they were carefully designed preparation for a divine assignment.

The Lord doesn't call the equipped; He equips the called. And He's been equipping you through every experience, every lesson, every victory, and yes, even every defeat. The refinement process has been intense because your calling is significant. Like Navy SEALs, Delta Force, or Army Rangers, you're being prepared for missions that others cannot undertake—spiritual operations in these last days that require exceptional preparation.

Remember that your training, while rigorous, is evidence of God's confidence in you. He believes in your capacity to fulfill the assignment He's prepared for you. He has invested heavily in your development because He sees the warrior you are becoming.

Reflection

Reflect on the challenging experiences in your life that have shaped you. Rather than viewing them as setbacks or punishments, recognize them as specialized training. What skills have you developed through adversity? What spiritual muscles have been strengthened? How has your endurance increased?

Action

Make a list of the specific ways God has trained you through life experiences—patience developed through waiting, compassion grown through suffering, faith strengthened through uncertainty. Thank Him specifically for each element of your training.

Prayer

Heavenly Father, thank You for the specialized training You've been providing for me. I recognize now that nothing in my life has been wasted—every experience has been preparation for my divine assignment. Help me to embrace even the difficult parts of my training with gratitude, knowing that You are developing in me the specific skills and strengths I'll need for the days ahead. Thank You for seeing in me what I often cannot see in myself. Complete the good work You've begun in me, Lord, and prepare me fully for the mission You've designed me to fulfill. In Jesus' name, Amen.

Journal

_____

_____

_____

_____

_____

_____

_____

_____

_____

_____

_____

_____

_____

_____

_____

_____

_____

_____

_____

_____

_____

_____

_____

_____

_____

_____

_____

_____

_____

_____

_____

_____

_____

_____

_____

_____

"Put on the whole armor of God, that you may be able to stand against the wiles of the devil. For we do not wrestle against flesh and blood, but against principalities, against powers, against the rulers of the darkness of this age, against spiritual hosts of wickedness in the heavenly places. Therefore take up the whole armor of God, that you may be able to withstand in the evil day, and having done all, to stand. Stand therefore, having girded your waist with truth, having put on the breastplate of righteousness, and having shod your feet with the preparation of the gospel of peace; above all, taking the shield of faith with which you will be able to quench all the fiery darts of the wicked one. And take the helmet of salvation, and the sword of the Spirit, which is the word of God; praying always with all prayer and supplication in the Spirit, being watchful to this end with all perseverance and supplication for all the saints."

Ephesians 6:11-18 (NKJV)

TODAY'S AFFIRMATIONS

I am equipped with God's mighty armor.

In Christ, I have everything I need to stand firm against every spiritual attack.

THE WARRIOR'S MINDSET

DAY 8: He Wears The Armor of God – 24/7

The spiritual battle we face requires divine protection. God has not left us defenseless but has provided us with spiritual armor that enables us to stand firm against every assault of the enemy. Each piece of this armor represents an aspect of Christ's character and the resources He makes available to us. When we put on this armor, we are essentially clothing ourselves with Christ Himself.

Reflection

Take inventory of your spiritual armor today. Are there pieces you've neglected? Perhaps you've set aside the shield of faith during times of doubt, or you've forgotten to wield the sword of the Spirit by neglecting God's Word.

Action

Intentionally "put on" each piece through prayer, affirming your reliance on God's protection.

ARMOR OF GOD

BELT OF TRUTH   BREAST PLATE OF RIGHTEOUSNESS   SHOES OF PEACE   SHIELD OF FAITH   HELMET OF SALVATION   SWORD OF SPIRIT

Prayer

Heavenly Father, I acknowledge that I am engaged in spiritual warfare. Thank You for providing the armor I need to stand firm. Help me to daily clothe myself with truth, righteousness, peace, faith, salvation, and Your Word. Teach me to pray persistently in the Spirit. I put on Christ Himself as my ultimate protection. In Jesus' name, Amen.

Journal

_____

_____

_____

_____

_____

_____

_____

_____

_____

_____

_____

_____

_____

_____

_____

_____

_____

_____

"For you died, and your life is hidden
with Christ in God."
Colossians 3:3 (NKJV)

TODAY'S AFFIRMATIONS

My life is hidden with Christ in God.

I am safely encompassed by divine protection, living from a place of heavenly security.

THE WARRIOR'S MINDSET

DAY 9: He is Hidden in Christ

When we come to Christ, something miraculous happens—our old self dies, and our new life becomes supernaturally hidden in Christ. You are invisible. This sacred concealment offers both protection and a new identity. The world may not recognize who we truly are because our real life is now wrapped up in Christ, safely tucked away in God Himself. This hidden position doesn't make us ineffective; rather, it gives us access to resources and power beyond human understanding.

Reflection

Rest in the security of being hidden in Christ today. When criticism, persecution, or spiritual attacks come your way, remember that your true identity and worth cannot be touched—they are safely concealed in Christ.

Action

From this position of security, you can operate with confidence, knowing that nothing can separate you from God's love and purpose for your life.

Prayer

Lord Jesus, thank You for the privilege of being hidden in You. Help me to daily embrace my death to self and my new life in You. When I feel exposed to the world's attacks, remind me that my true identity is safely concealed in Your presence. Let me live from this place of security and confidence. In Jesus' name, Amen.

Journal

_____

_____

_____

_____

_____

_____

_____

_____

_____

_____

_____

_____

_____

_____

_____

_____

_____

_____

_____

_____

_____

_____

_____

_____

_____

_____

_____

_____

_____

_____

_____

_____

_____

_____

_____

_____

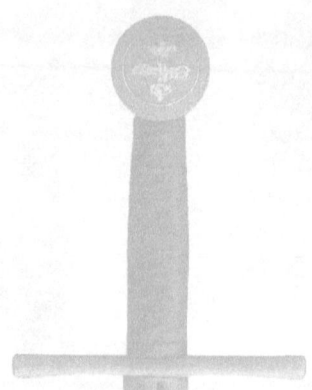

"To them God willed to make known what are the riches of the glory of this mystery among the Gentiles: which is Christ in you, the hope of glory."
Colossians 1:27 (NKJV)

TODAY'S AFFIRMATIONS

Christ lives in me.

His presence is my strength, my wisdom, and my hope of reflecting God's glory to the world.

THE WARRIOR'S MINDSET

DAY 10: Christ in Him is the Hope of Glory

The indwelling presence of Christ is the greatest mystery and miracle of our faith. The Creator of the universe has chosen to make His home within us! This indwelling presence is not just a theological concept but the very source of our transformation and our only genuine hope for reflecting God's glory. Christ in us generates power for living, wisdom for decisions, and character that increasingly resembles Him.

Reflection

Take a moment today to acknowledge Christ's presence within you. Instead of trying to overcome challenges through your own strength or wisdom, consciously rely on Christ's indwelling power.

Action

Practice this awareness by pausing throughout the day to say, "Christ in me is my hope for handling this situation with glory."

Prayer

Lord Jesus, I stand amazed that You have chosen to dwell within me. Forgive me for the times I've tried to live independently of Your indwelling presence. Help me to be constantly aware that You are in me, providing everything I need for life and godliness. Let Your life within me radiate outward so others can see Your glory. In Jesus' name, Amen.

Journal

_____

_____

_____

_____

_____

_____

_____

_____

_____

_____

_____

_____

_____

_____

_____

_____

_____

_____

_____

_____

_____

_____

_____

_____

_____

_____

_____

_____

_____

_____

_____

_____

_____

_____

_____

"I have been crucified with Christ; it is no longer I who live, but Christ lives in me; and the life which I now live in the flesh I live by faith in the Son of God, who loved me and gave Himself for me."
Galatians 2:20 (NKJV)

TODAY'S AFFIRMATIONS

I have been crucified with Christ.

My old self is dead, and now Christ lives in me.

By faith, I access His life and power for every situation I face.

THE WARRIOR'S
MINDSET

DAY 11: He Has Been Crucified with Christ

Through our identification with Christ, we have spiritually participated in His crucifixion. Our old self with its sinful desires and worldly ambitions has been put to death. This crucifixion with Christ is the gateway to experiencing His resurrection power. It means we no longer live for ourselves or by our own resources. Instead, Christ Himself becomes our life source, and we learn to live by faith in Him.

Reflection

Consider what aspects of your old self might still be demanding life today. Are there sinful habits, selfish ambitions, or worldly values that you need to reckon as dead through your identification with Christ's crucifixion?

Action

Choose to live today by faith in Christ rather than by your own strength, allowing His life to flow through you to accomplish what you never could on your own.

Prayer

Heavenly Father, thank You for including me in Christ's death so that I might share in His life. Help me to daily reckon myself dead to sin but alive to You. When my old nature tries to reassert itself, remind me that it has been crucified with Christ. Teach me to live by faith in Your Son, drawing on His life within me for everything I need. In Jesus' name, Amen.

Journal

_____

_____

_____

_____

_____

_____

_____

_____

_____

_____

_____

_____

_____

_____

_____

_____

_____

_____

_____

_____

_____

_____

_____

_____

_____

_____

_____

_____

_____

_____

_____

_____

_____

_____

_____

_____

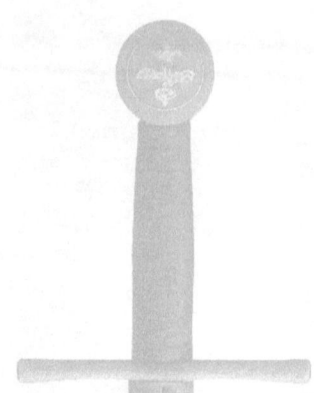

"Behold, I give you the authority to trample on serpents and scorpions, and over all the power of the enemy, and nothing shall by any means hurt you."
Luke 10:19 (NKJV)

TODAY'S AFFIRMATIONS

I have been given authority by Jesus Christ Himself.

I stand against evil, pray with confidence, and advance God's kingdom through His power working in me.

THE WARRIOR'S MINDSET

DAY 12: He Has Been Given All Power and Authority

As believers, we have been granted spiritual authority that comes directly from Jesus Christ. This isn't about personal power or control but about representing the Kingdom of God with the delegated authority of its King. This authority enables us to resist and overcome evil forces, to pray effectively, and to advance God's kingdom. Just as an ambassador carries the authority of their country, we carry Christ's authority in spiritual matters.

Reflection

Where do you need to exercise the spiritual authority Christ has given you today? Perhaps there's a persistent temptation you need to resist, a spiritual stronghold that needs to be broken, or a kingdom mission that requires bold action.

Action

Approach these situations with the confident humility of one who has been delegated authority from the King of kings.

Prayer

Lord Jesus, thank You for entrusting me with Your authority over all the power of the enemy. Help me to exercise this authority with humility and wisdom, never for selfish gain but always for Your glory and the advancement of Your kingdom. Where evil resists, give me courage to stand firm in the authority You have given me. In Jesus' name, Amen.

Journal

_____

_____

_____

_____

_____

_____

_____

_____

_____

_____

_____

_____

_____

_____

_____

_____

_____

_____

"And the LORD, He is the One who goes before you. He will be with you, He will not leave you nor forsake you; do not fear nor be dismayed."
Deuteronomy 31:8 (NKJV)

TODAY'S AFFIRMATIONS

The Lord goes before me and remains with me.

I need not fear, for my divine Commander has already secured my victory.

THE WARRIOR'S MINDSET

DAY 13: He Knows His Commander Has Already Gone Before Him

We never face any battle alone or unprepared. Our divine Commander, the Lord Himself, always goes ahead of us, preparing the way and ensuring victory. This doesn't mean we won't face struggles, but it does mean the outcome is already secured. Jesus has already conquered every enemy we will ever face. Like a good military leader, He doesn't send us where He hasn't been, and He remains with us through every conflict.

Reflection

What challenges are you facing today that seem overwhelming?

Action

Remember that the Lord has already gone before you into these situations. He has prepared the way and secured the victory. Let this truth dissolve your fear and strengthen your resolve. Move forward with confidence, knowing your Commander has already charted the path to success.

Prayer

Lord, thank You for going before me in every battle I face. When I feel afraid or uncertain, remind me that You have already been where I am going and have prepared the way. Help me to follow confidently where You lead, knowing that You will never leave me nor forsake me. I trust in Your victorious presence. In Jesus' name, Amen.

Journal

_____

_____

_____

_____

_____

_____

_____

_____

_____

_____

_____

_____

_____

_____

_____

_____

_____

_____

_____

_____

_____

_____

_____

_____

_____

_____

_____

_____

_____

_____

_____

_____

_____

_____

_____

_____

_____

_____

"That I may know Him and the power of His resurrection, and the fellowship of His sufferings, being conformed to His death."
Philippians 3:10 (NKJV)

TODAY'S AFFIRMATIONS

I embrace both the power of Christ's resurrection and the fellowship of His sufferings.

These shared experiences are privileges that deepen my knowledge of Him.

THE WARRIOR'S
MINDSET

DAY 14: He Considers Suffering for Christ an Honor and A Privilege

Paul reveals a profound spiritual insight—knowing Christ intimately involves both the power of His resurrection and the fellowship of His sufferings. There is a depth of relationship with Jesus that can only be accessed through shared suffering. Suffering, death, and resurrection are experiences the end-times warrior has had often and considers privileges.

When we suffer for Christ or like Christ, we enter into a special communion with Him. This is not about seeking pain, but recognizing that our sufferings can become sacred spaces of intimacy with our Savior, ultimately conforming us to His image.

Reflection

How are you currently experiencing suffering in your life?

Action

Instead of merely enduring it or questioning why it's happening, consider it an opportunity for deeper fellowship with Christ. Ask Him to meet you in your pain and reveal Himself to you in new ways. Look for how your current struggles might be conforming you to Christ's death—perhaps by dying to self-reliance, pride, or worldly security—so that you might also experience the power of His resurrection.

Prayer

Lord Jesus, I confess that I typically try to avoid suffering rather than seeing it as a pathway to knowing You more deeply. Help me to embrace the fellowship of Your sufferings when they come, recognizing them as opportunities for intimate communion with You. In my current trials, meet me in powerful ways and conform me to Your death, that I might also experience the power of Your resurrection. In Jesus' name, Amen.

Journal

_____

_____

_____

_____

_____

_____

_____

_____

_____

_____

_____

_____

_____

_____

_____

_____

_____

_____

_____

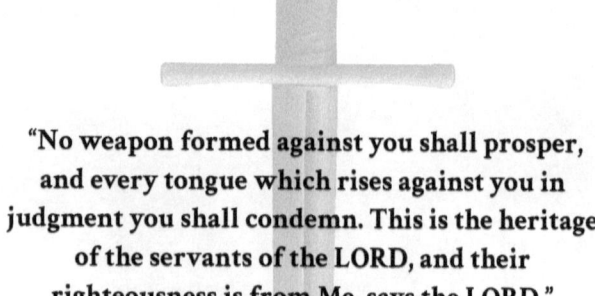

"No weapon formed against you shall prosper, and every tongue which rises against you in judgment you shall condemn. This is the heritage of the servants of the LORD, and their righteousness is from Me, says the LORD."
Isaiah 54:17 (NKJV)

TODAY'S AFFIRMATIONS

No weapon formed against me shall prosper.

My security and vindication come from the Lord.

I stand protected as His servant.

THE WARRIOR'S MINDSET

DAY 15: He is Invincible in Christ

God promises a remarkable defensive covering over His people. While weapons may be formed and attacks may come, they will not ultimately succeed in their destructive purpose. This doesn't mean we won't be targeted or temporarily wounded, but rather that no attack can thwart God's ultimate purpose for our lives. Our vindication and protection come from the Lord Himself, making this security our rightful inheritance as His servants.

Reflection

Identify the "weapons" currently formed against you— whether they're physical threats, relational conflicts, financial pressures, or spiritual attacks.

Action

Now, instead of being overwhelmed by these challenges, declare God's promise over each situation. Your ultimate victory doesn't depend on your strength or strategy but on God's faithful promise that these weapons will not prosper against you.

Prayer

Heavenly Father, thank You for Your promise that no weapon formed against me shall prosper. When I face attacks from every direction, help me to stand firm in this truth. I declare that my righteousness and vindication come from You alone. Though enemies may form weapons, I trust in Your superior protection and Your perfect plan for my life. In Jesus' name, Amen.

Journal

_____

_____

_____

_____

_____

_____

_____

_____

_____

_____

_____

_____

_____

_____

_____

_____

_____

_____

"Being confident of this very thing, that He
who has begun a good work in you will
complete it until the day of Jesus Christ."
Philippians 1:6 (NKJV)

"Now may our Lord Jesus Christ Himself, and our God
and Father, who has loved us and given us everlasting
consolation and good hope by grace, comfort your hearts
and establish you in every good word and work."
2 Thessalonians 2:16-17 (NKJV)

TODAY'S AFFIRMATION
I am specially trained, divinely equipped, and purposefully prepared by God Himself for the mission He has assigned to me.

THE WARRIOR'S MINDSET

DAY 16: He is Divinely Equipped For His Calling

A warrior's effectiveness depends largely on their training and equipment. As spiritual warriors, we have the ultimate advantage—we have been especially trained, equipped, and prepared by our Commander Himself. God doesn't send us into battle unprepared. Every experience, every lesson, every victory, and every defeat in your life has been part of your divine preparation for the mission He has assigned to you.

The confidence we carry into our mission comes not from our own abilities but from the certainty that God Himself has begun this good work in us, and He will faithfully complete it. This training isn't generic but personal and specialized. The Master Craftsman is shaping you with precision, developing in you exactly what you need for the specific assignment He has for you. And He doesn't simply train you and send you off alone—He establishes you, supports you, and empowers you in every good word and work.

Reflection

Consider your unique combination of talents, experiences, and even wounds. How might God be using these as specialized training for your specific calling?

Action

Take time to list three aspects of your life story that seemed difficult or even meaningless at the time, but now reveal themselves as preparation for your current ministry or challenges. Ask God to show you how He is currently equipping you for future assignments.

Prayer

Heavenly Father, thank You for the personal attention You've given to my training and preparation. I am humbled to think that You, the Creator of the universe, have specifically equipped me for service in Your kingdom. When I feel inadequate for the tasks before me, remind me that You have prepared me for this very moment. Thank You for Your promise to complete the good work You've begun in me. I trust in Your perfect training program for my life. Establish me in every good word and work according to Your purpose. In Jesus' name, Amen.

Journal

_____

_____

_____

_____

_____

_____

_____

_____

_____

_____

_____

_____

_____

_____

_____

_____

_____

_____

_____

_____

_____

_____

_____

_____

_____

_____

_____

_____

_____

_____

_____

_____

_____

_____

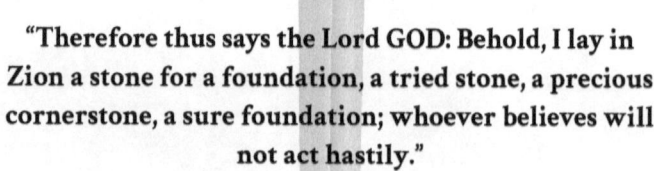

"Therefore thus says the Lord GOD: Behold, I lay in Zion a stone for a foundation, a tried stone, a precious cornerstone, a sure foundation; whoever believes will not act hastily."
Isaiah 28:16 (NKJV)

"If indeed you have tasted that the Lord is gracious. Coming to Him as to a living stone, rejected indeed by men, but chosen by God and precious, you also, as living stones, are being built up a spiritual house, a holy priesthood, to offer up spiritual sacrifices acceptable to God through Jesus Christ."
1 Peter 2:3-5 (NKJV)

TODAY'S AFFIRMATIONS

I am a living stone in God's temple, carefully chosen and precisely placed.

My life has eternal significance as part of His divine structure.

THE WARRIOR'S MINDSET

DAY 17: His is One of Many Living Stones

Christ is the cornerstone upon which God's kingdom is built. As believers, we too are living stones, carefully positioned by the Master Builder to create a spiritual temple where God dwells. Each of us has a unique and irreplaceable position in this divine structure. We find our true purpose and meaning when we recognize our connection to Christ and our fellow believers in this spiritual building.

Reflection

Consider your place in God's spiritual house today. How are you contributing to the beauty and strength of His temple?

Action

Remember that you are not meant to stand alone but to be joined with other believers, all connected to Christ, the cornerstone. Think about how your life, talents, and spiritual gifts fit into God's greater design.

Prayer

Lord Jesus, thank You for being the cornerstone of my faith. Help me to find my rightful place in Your spiritual house. Shape me and position me according to Your perfect design. May I stand firm upon You, connected to my brothers and sisters in faith, to create a dwelling place worthy of Your presence. In Jesus' name, Amen.

Journal

_____

_____

_____

_____

_____

_____

_____

_____

_____

_____

_____

_____

_____

_____

_____

_____

_____

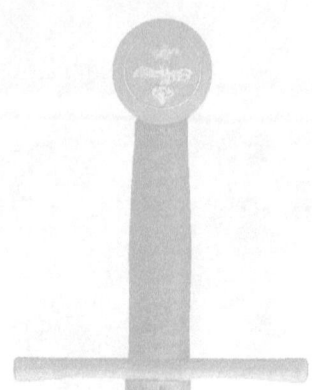

"These things I have spoken to you, that in Me you may have peace. In the world you will have tribulation; but be of good cheer, I have overcome the world."
John 16:33 (NKJV)

TODAY'S AFFIRMATIONS

I fight from a position of victory because Christ has already overcome the world.

I can face tribulation with peace and joy, knowing the final outcome is secure.

THE WARRIOR'S MINDSET

DAY 18: He Lives In The Peace Of God

Jesus doesn't minimize the reality of our struggles—He acknowledges that in this world, we will face tribulation. Yet He offers an even greater reality: He has already overcome the world! This means that every battle we fight has already been decisively won by Christ. We're not fighting for victory; we're fighting from victory. This profound truth infuses our struggles with hope and allows us to face tribulation with genuine joy and peace.

Reflection

What tribulation are you currently experiencing?

Action

Instead of seeing it only as a painful struggle, reframe it as an opportunity to participate in and demonstrate Christ's already-secured victory. Approach your challenges today with the confidence and peace that come from knowing the ultimate outcome has already been determined by Christ's triumph.

Prayer

Lord Jesus, thank You for overcoming the world and securing victory on my behalf. When tribulation comes, help me remember that You have already won the battle. Fill me with Your peace and joy even in the midst of struggles. May I live as one who knows the end of the story—that Your victory is certain and will ultimately be revealed in every area of my life. In Jesus' name, Amen.

Journal

_____

_____

_____

_____

_____

_____

_____

_____

_____

_____

_____

_____

_____

_____

_____

_____

_____

_____

"Then Peter said, See, we have left all and followed You."
Luke 18:28 (NKJV)

TODAY'S AFFIRMATIONS

I have decided to follow Jesus, no turning back.

He is my greatest treasure, worth any sacrifice I could make.

THE WARRIOR'S MINDSET

DAY 19: He Follows Christ at All Cost

The authentic Christian journey involves sacrifice. Like the disciples who left their livelihoods, comfort, and security to follow Jesus, we too are called to release whatever hinders wholehearted devotion to Christ. This letting go isn't about earning God's favor but about removing distractions and competitors for our affection and allegiance. When we willingly release what the world holds dear, we discover that Christ is more than enough—indeed, He is the pearl of great price worth everything we could surrender.

Reflection

Take an honest inventory today: What are you still clinging to that might be hindering your full surrender to Christ? Perhaps it's material security, reputation, comfort, or even good things that have become ultimate things.

Action

Ask the Holy Spirit to reveal any area where you need to loosen your grip in order to more fully grasp Christ and His kingdom.

Prayer

Lord Jesus, like Peter and the other disciples, I want to be able to say I have left all to follow You. Show me where I'm still holding back or clinging to things that compete with my devotion to You. Give me courage to release whatever You highlight, trusting that You are worth far more than anything I could surrender. Help me to follow You with an undivided heart. In Jesus' name, Amen.

Journal

"But thanks be to God, who gives us the
victory through our Lord Jesus Christ."
1 Corinthians 15:57 (NKJV)

"For whatever is born of God overcomes the world . And
this is the victory that has overcome the world—our faith."
1 John 5:4 (NKJV)

"And I saw something like a sea of glass mingled with
fire, and those who have the victory over the beast, over
his image and over his mark and over the number of his
name, standing on the sea of glass, having harps of God."
Revelation 15:2 (NKJV)

TODAY'S AFFIRMATIONS

The victory is already mine through Christ Jesus.

I fight from a position of triumph, overcoming the world
through my faith.

THE WARRIOR'S MINDSET

DAY 20: He Rests Assured of Christ's Victory

The Christian doesn't fight to win but from a position of already having won through Christ. This revolutionary perspective transforms how we approach spiritual warfare and life's challenges. Victory isn't something we achieve through our efforts; it's something God gives us through Jesus Christ. Our faith connects us to this victory, allowing us to overcome the world with its temptations and threats. Even in the end times, believers are depicted as those who have gained victory over every evil system through their faith in Christ.

Reflection

Instead of striving anxiously or fighting desperately, stand firmly in the triumph Christ has already secured. When temptation, opposition, or spiritual warfare arises, respond not as one fighting for victory but as one who already possesses it through Christ. This posture of confident faith is itself an act of victory over the enemy.

Action

Approach today's challenges from a victory mindset.

Prayer

Heavenly Father, thank You for giving me victory through my Lord Jesus Christ. Help me to fully grasp and live from this position of triumph. When battles come, remind me that the victory is already mine through Christ. Strengthen my faith to overcome the world with all its temptations and threats. May I live today as one who knows the final outcome—standing victorious with all the saints. In Jesus' name, Amen.

Journal

"And being found in appearance as a man, He humbled Himself and became obedient to the point of death, even the death of the cross."
Philippians 2:8 (NKJV)

TODAY'S AFFIRMATIONS

I am committed to following Christ in complete obedience, regardless of the cost.

His path of surrender is my path to abundant life.

THE WARRIOR'S MINDSET

DAY 21: He Follows Christ's Example of Obedience

Christ's ultimate expression of love and obedience to the Father was His willingness to die. Following Jesus means adopting this same radical commitment—being willing to obey God regardless of the cost, even to the point of death if necessary. This doesn't mean we seek suffering, but we value obedience to God above self-preservation. This level of surrender unleashes God's power in extraordinary ways, just as Christ's obedience unto death led to His resurrection and exaltation.

Reflection

What is God asking of you that seems too costly or difficult? Where are you hesitating to fully obey because of potential loss or suffering?

Action

Consider Christ's example and ask for grace to follow Him in complete obedience, regardless of the personal cost. Remember that the path of self-denial, though challenging, leads to resurrection life and spiritual fruitfulness.

Prayer

Lord Jesus, I am humbled by Your example of obedience unto death. Forgive me for the times I've chosen self-preservation over full obedience to the Father. Grant me the courage to follow You regardless of the cost, knowing that the path of surrender leads to resurrection power. Help me to hold my very life with open hands, willing to lay it down if that's what obedience requires. In Jesus' name, Amen.

Journal

_____

_____

_____

_____

_____

_____

_____

_____

_____

_____

_____

_____

_____

_____

_____

_____

_____

_____

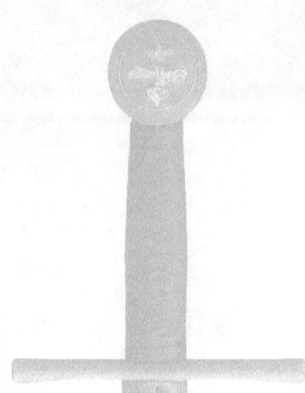

> "Teaching them to observe all things that I have commanded you; and lo, I am with you always, even to the end of the age."
> Matthew 28:20 (NKJV)

TODAY'S AFFIRMATIONS

Jesus Christ is with me always.

I am never alone, not even for a moment.

His presence accompanies me in every circumstance of life.

THE WARRIOR'S MINDSET

DAY 22: He Knows He Is Never Alone

Jesus' parting promise to His disciples carries profound implications for every believer. We are never alone. The risen Christ accompanies us through every situation—the triumphant and the tragic, the ordinary and the overwhelming. His presence doesn't guarantee an absence of difficulty, but it ensures we never face any circumstance without divine companionship and support. This promise extends "to the end of the age," meaning there is no moment in time when His presence isn't available to us.

Reflection

When anxiety or loneliness threaten, what is your first response?

Action

Practice awareness of Christ's presence today. In each meeting, conversation, challenge, or blessing, consciously acknowledge that Jesus is present with you. Let this awareness shape how you respond to difficulties (you're not facing them alone) and how you celebrate joys (sharing them with the One who loves you most).

Prayer

Lord Jesus, thank You for Your promise to be with me always, even to the end of the age. Forgive me for the times I've lived as though I were alone, facing challenges and celebrations without acknowledging Your presence. Increase my awareness of Your companionship throughout this day. In moments of struggle, remind me that You are with me. In moments of joy, let me sense You rejoicing alongside me. In Jesus' name, Amen.

Journal

_____

_____

_____

_____

_____

_____

_____

_____

_____

_____

_____

_____

_____

_____

_____

_____

_____

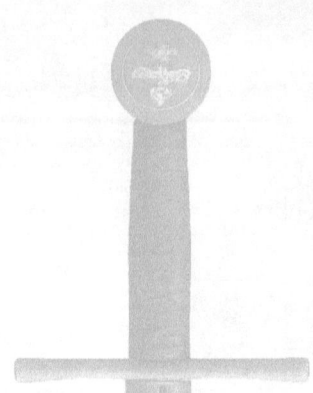

"Beloved, do not think it strange concerning
the fiery trial which is to try you, as though some
strange thing happened to you;"
1 Peter 4:12 (NKJV)

TODAY'S AFFIRMATIONS

My present challenges are divine training exercises, preparing
me for greater spiritual realities.

I will embrace them as preparation for the battles ahead.

THE WARRIOR'S
MINDSET

DAY 23: He Has Been Trained with Eternity in Mind

The trials, tests, and challenges we face in our earthly life serve as preparation for greater spiritual realities. Like military training exercises that simulate battlefield conditions, our current struggles develop the spiritual muscles and reflexes we'll need for the actual warfare ahead. This perspective helps us approach difficulties not as meaningless suffering but as purposeful preparation. Like elite soldiers who undergo rigorous training, we can embrace hardship knowing it's developing our spiritual readiness for what lies ahead.

Reflection

Consider your current challenges as spiritual training exercises rather than pointless ordeals. What spiritual muscles is God developing in you through these difficulties? How might your present struggles be preparing you for future kingdom service?

Action

Approach today's "training simulations" with the seriousness of one preparing for actual combat, knowing that your Coach is intentionally equipping you for greater battles ahead.

Prayer

Heavenly Father, help me to see my current trials as training for greater spiritual realities. When I'm tempted to view my struggles as meaningless or overwhelming, remind me that You are using them to prepare me for what lies ahead. Give me the endurance of a soldier in training, willing to embrace difficulty for the sake of future effectiveness. Thank You for being my faithful Trainer, developing in me what I'll need for the battles to come. In Jesus' name, Amen.

Journal

_____

_____

_____

_____

_____

_____

_____

_____

_____

_____

_____

_____

_____

_____

_____

_____

_____

"Who makes His angels spirits, His
ministers a flame of fire."
Psalm 104:4 (NKJV)

"And of the angels He says: 'Who makes His angels
spirits and His ministers a flame of fire."
Hebrews 1:7 (NKJV)

TODAY'S AFFIRMATIONS

The fire of God Himself burns in my heart.

I am His minister—a flame of fire bringing light, warmth, and
transformation wherever I go.

THE WARRIOR'S MINDSET

DAY 24: His Heart Is On Fire

God describes His servants—His ministers—as flames of fire. This is no casual metaphor but a profound revelation of how God intends His warriors to function in this world. Fire is a powerful force: it illuminates darkness, consumes what is worthless, purifies what is valuable, provides warmth to the cold, and spreads with uncontainable energy. When the fire of God Himself burns in your heart, you become a transformative presence wherever you go.

This divine fire is not of our own kindling. It is God's very presence burning within us—His passion, His purpose, His power. Like the burning bush Moses encountered, we become vessels ablaze with divine presence yet not consumed by it. This holy fire purifies our own motives and desires while simultaneously igniting others with the truth and love of God.

Reflection

Reflect on the intensity of your spiritual fire. Has it dimmed to glowing embers, or is it burning brightly? What might be smothering your flame—complacency, discouragement, fear, or sin?

Action

Take time today to stoke the fire through worship, prayer, and meditation on God's Word. Ask God to reveal specific areas where your particular "flame" can bring light, warmth, and transformation to those around you.

Prayer

Holy Spirit, kindle afresh Your sacred fire within me. Burn away anything that doesn't reflect Your glory. Let Your consuming fire ignite my passion, purify my heart, and illuminate the path before me. May I be recognized as Your minister—a flame of fire bringing Your presence into every dark place. Make me bold to spread Your light without fear of being extinguished. Let the fire of God Himself burn so brightly in my heart that others are drawn to its warmth and light. In Jesus' name, Amen.

Journal

_____

_____

_____

_____

_____

_____

_____

_____

_____

_____

_____

_____

_____

_____

_____

_____

_____

_____

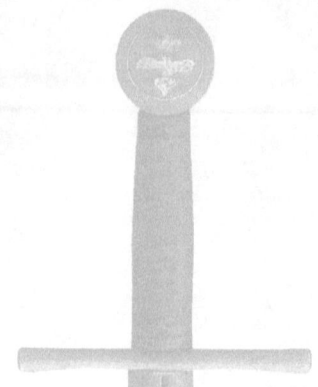

**"Not with eyeservice, as men-pleasers,
but as bondservants of Christ, doing the
will of God from the heart."**
Ephesians 6:6 (NKJV)

TODAY'S AFFIRMATIONS

My sole desire is to please God, not man.

I will serve with sincerity of heart, knowing that the only opinion that truly matters is His.

THE WARRIOR'S MINDSET

DAY 25: His Heart Is to Please The King

The warrior of God understands that there is only one opinion that truly matters—the opinion of the Commander. In a world filled with pressures to conform to human expectations, we are called to a higher standard: pleasing God alone. This distinction is crucial. Men-pleasers serve vigorously when others are watching but slack when alone. God-pleasers maintain unwavering devotion whether in public or private because they serve from the heart.

Living to please God alone liberates us from the exhausting need for human approval. No longer must we adjust our convictions to match popular opinion or fear the criticism that comes with bold obedience. When pleasing God becomes our sole desire, we find a paradoxical freedom—we are bound to Christ yet more liberated than ever before. Our sole desire becomes doing the will of God from the heart, regardless of who applauds or who criticizes.

Reflection

Examine your motivations in your work, ministry, or relationships. Are you performing for human approval or serving from a heart devoted to God? Identify one area where you've been especially concerned with others' opinions and consciously surrender it to God today.

Action

Practice doing one good deed that no one but God will see, reinforcing your commitment to please Him alone.

Prayer

Heavenly Father, forgive me for the times I've served with divided loyalties, seeking human approval above Your pleasure. Purify my heart so that I might serve You with undistracted devotion. Free me from the fear of human opinion and the addiction to human praise. Let my sole desire be to please You, whether others notice or not, whether they approve or not. May I do Your will from the heart, finding my identity and satisfaction in You alone. In Jesus' name, Amen.

Journal

_____

_____

_____

_____

_____

_____

_____

_____

_____

_____

_____

_____

_____

_____

_____

_____

_____

_____

_____

"For the eyes of the LORD run to and fro throughout
the whole earth, to show Himself strong on
behalf of those whose heart is loyal to Him."
2 Chronicles 16:9 (NKJV)

"The eyes of the LORD are on the righteous,
and His ears are open to their cry."
Psalm 34:15 (NKJV)

TODAY'S AFFIRMATIONS

I am carefully watched by my Commander.

His eyes are upon me to strengthen, protect, and guide me in
every situation.

THE WARRIOR'S MINDSET

DAY 26: He Knows God is Watching Him

Imagine a warrior fighting valiantly on the battlefield, unaware that his commander watches from a nearby hill, ready to send reinforcements at the critical moment. How much more confidently would that warrior fight if he knew he was being carefully observed? This is our reality as spiritual warriors—we serve under the watchful eye of our Commander.

God's watchful gaze is not one of critical inspection but of loving attention. His eyes search for opportunities to show Himself strong on our behalf. He sees your faithful service in obscure places. He notices your loyalty when others have abandoned the post. He watches your struggles, not as a distant observer, but as a Commander intimately involved in your battle, whose ears are attentive to your every cry.

Reflection

Consider how your actions might change if you maintained constant awareness of God's attentive gaze.

Action

Practice this awareness today by periodically pausing to acknowledge His presence. When facing difficult decisions or temptations, remind yourself: "The eyes of the Lord are upon me." When feeling discouraged or overlooked, remember: "God sees my faithfulness and will strengthen me."

Prayer

Sovereign Lord, thank You for Your constant, watchful care over my life. Help me to live with the conscious awareness that Your eyes are always upon me—not to condemn but to protect and provide. When I feel alone in the battle, remind me that You see every step I take. When I am tempted to compromise, help me remember Your attentive gaze. Thank You that Your watchfulness means I am never forgotten, never abandoned, and never without help in times of need. May I live worthy of Your watchful eye today. In Jesus' name, Amen.

Journal

_____

_____

_____

_____

_____

_____

_____

_____

_____

_____

_____

_____

_____

_____

_____

_____

_____

"Are not five sparrows sold for two copper coins?
And not one of them is forgotten before God."
Luke 12:6 (NKJV)

"But the very hairs of your head are all numbered.
Do not fear therefore; you are of more value
than many sparrows."
Luke 12:7 (NKJV)

TODAY'S AFFIRMATIONS

My value is greater than many sparrows.

I am specifically known, personally loved, and infinitely trea-
sured by God Himself.

THE WARRIOR'S MINDSET

DAY 27: He is Valued Beyond Measure

In ancient times, sparrows were among the least valuable creatures—sold cheaply in the marketplace as food for the poor. Yet Jesus reveals an astonishing truth: not one of these seemingly insignificant birds is forgotten before God. How much more, then, does He value you—created in His image, redeemed by His Son's blood, and called to eternal partnership with Him?

Your value to God is not based on your performance, position, or productivity. It is intrinsic to who you are as His beloved creation. The same God who tracks the flight of every sparrow has counted every hair on your head—such is the detail of His care for you. This intimate knowledge is not meant to make us feel scrutinized but deeply cherished. The Creator of the universe treasures you personally, specifically, and endlessly.

Reflection

Take a moment to consider how you measure your own worth. Are you valuing yourself by the world's standards of achievement, appearance, or acclaim? Or by God's standard of inherent, immeasurable worth? Choose one area where you've felt "less than" and deliberately replace that lie with the truth of your value to God.

Action

Look for opportunities today to affirm the God-given worth of others who may feel overlooked or undervalued.

Prayer

Loving Father, thank You for the reminder that I am valued beyond measure in Your sight. When I feel insignificant or forgotten, help me remember that You track even the sparrows—and I am worth far more to You. Thank You for the intimate care that counts every hair on my head. Free me from seeking validation through human standards and help me rest secure in Your unchanging love. May I extend this same recognition of worth to everyone I encounter today. In Jesus' precious name, Amen.

Journal

_____

_____

_____

_____

_____

_____

_____

_____

_____

_____

_____

_____

_____

_____

_____

_____

_____

_____

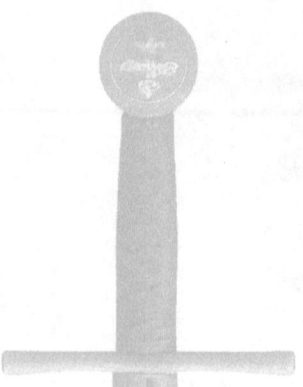

"Though I speak with the tongues of men and of angels, but have not love, I have become sounding brass or a clanging cymbal."
1 Corinthians 13:1 (NKJV)

"And above all things have fervent love for one another, for 'love will cover a multitude of sins."
1 Peter 4:8 (NKJV)

TODAY'S AFFIRMATIONS

Love motivates my actions and transforms my service.

I choose to relate to others from a place of genuine love rather than duty or self-interest.

THE WARRIOR'S MINDSET

DAY 28: He Is Motivated by Love

Love is not merely an emotion but the driving force behind all meaningful spiritual activity. Without love, even the most impressive spiritual gifts and actions become empty noise. God prioritizes the heart behind our actions over the actions themselves. When we allow love to be our primary motivation, it transforms not only what we do but how and why we do it. This fervent love has redemptive power, covering offenses and creating space for healing and reconciliation.

Reflection

Examine your motives today. Are your actions toward others—especially in challenging relationships—motivated by love or by obligation, fear, or self-interest?

Action

Choose one relationship or situation where you can intentionally act from a place of love rather than duty. Remember that love-motivated actions may look exactly the same outwardly as duty-motivated ones, but they carry a different spiritual weight and impact.

Prayer

Father, purify my motives and help me to act from genuine love rather than obligation or self-interest. Let Your love flow through me toward others, especially in difficult relationships. Show me where I've been operating without love, and transform those areas of my life. May everything I do today be motivated by and saturated with Your perfect love. In Jesus' name, Amen.

Journal

_____

_____

_____

_____

_____

_____

_____

_____

_____

_____

_____

_____

_____

_____

_____

_____

_____

_____

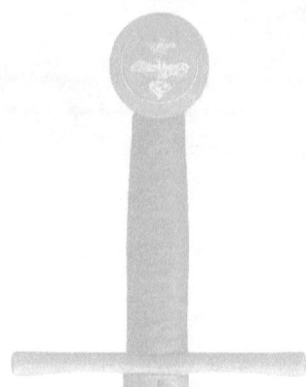

"The fear of the Lord is the instruction of wisdom, and before honor is humility."
Proverbs. 15:33 (NKJV)

"By humility and the fear of the Lord are riches and honor and life."
Proverbs 22:4 (NKJV)

"Likewise you younger people, submit yourselves to your elders. Yes, all of you be submissive to one another, and be clothed with humility, for 'God resists the proud, but gives grace to the humble."
Peter 5:5 (NKJV)

TODAY'S AFFIRMATIONS

I clothe myself in humility daily, receiving God's grace and favor.

I serve others without seeking recognition, knowing that true honor comes from God.

THE WARRIOR'S MINDSET

DAY 29: He Is Clothed In Humility

Scripture consistently presents humility as a prerequisite for God's favor and blessing. The image of being "clothed with humility" suggests that humility should be as visible and essential to our spiritual identity as the clothes we wear. True humility isn't self-deprecation but an accurate assessment of ourselves before God—recognizing both our dignity as His creation and our dependence on His grace. When we embrace humility, we position ourselves to receive God's grace and wisdom rather than His resistance.

Reflection

Consider where pride might be operating in your life—perhaps in relationships, at work, or in your spiritual journey.

Action

Practice "clothing yourself with humility" by deliberately choosing to serve others today without seeking recognition. Look for opportunities to defer to others' preferences or to acknowledge others' contributions before your own. Remember that humility isn't denying your strengths but using them with gratitude and for others' benefit.

Prayer

Lord, I confess the areas of pride in my life. Teach me what it means to be truly clothed in humility. Help me to see myself as You see me—neither inflating nor diminishing my worth and gifts. Give me the courage to serve without recognition and to submit to others in love. I want to position myself to receive Your grace rather than Your resistance. Make humility as natural to me as the clothes I wear. In Jesus' name, Amen.

Journal

_____

_____

_____

_____

_____

_____

_____

_____

_____

_____

_____

_____

_____

_____

_____

_____

_____

_____

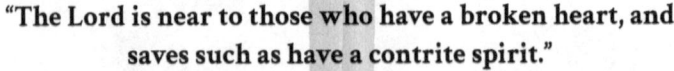

"The Lord is near to those who have a broken heart, and saves such as have a contrite spirit."
Psalm 34:18 (NKJV)

"The sacrifices of God are a broken spirit, a broken and a contrite heart—These, O God, You will not despise."
Psalm 51:17 (NKJV)

"For thus says the High and Lofty One Who inhabits eternity, whose name is Holy: I dwell in the high and holy place, with him who has a contrite and humble spirit, to revive the spirit of the humble, and to revive the heart of the contrite ones."
Isaiah 57:15 (NKJV)

TODAY'S AFFIRMATIONS

I approach God with a broken and contrite heart, knowing He is near to me in my brokenness.

My vulnerability before God becomes the place of His restoration and presence.

THE WARRIOR'S MINDSET

DAY 30: He Offers God His Broken Heart

The counterintuitive reality of the spiritual life is that brokenness before God leads to wholeness. A broken heart—one that is tender, repentant, and aware of its need for God—creates space for divine encounter. Rather than being repelled by our brokenness, God is actually drawn to it. He promises not just His presence but His reviving power to those who approach Him with genuine contrition and humility. This brokenness isn't about self-loathing but about honest recognition of our spiritual condition and complete dependence on God.

Reflection

Rather than hiding your failures, weaknesses, or pain from God, bring them honestly before Him today. Practice spiritual vulnerability by acknowledging specific areas where you need God's healing and transformation.

Action

Consider journaling a heartfelt prayer of confession and dependence. Remember that a broken heart before God isn't the end of the story but the beginning of restoration and intimacy with Him.

Prayer

Holy God, I come before You with a broken and contrite heart. I acknowledge my failures, weaknesses, and complete dependence on You. Thank You that You don't despise my brokenness but are drawn to it. I invite Your reviving presence into the broken places of my life. Restore me, heal me, and use even my failures to draw me closer to You. Make me tender-hearted toward You and others. I trust that in my brokenness, I will find Your wholeness. In Jesus' name, Amen.

Journal

_____

_____

_____

_____

_____

_____

_____

_____

_____

_____

_____

_____

_____

_____

_____

_____

_____

"But the hour is coming, and now is, when the true worshipers will worship the Father in spirit and truth; for the Father is seeking such to worship Him. God is Spirit, and those who worship Him must worship in spirit and truth."
John 4:23-24 (NKJV)

"And now my head shall be lifted up above my enemies all around me; Therefore I will offer sacrifices of joy in His tabernacle; I will sing, yes, I will sing praises to the Lord."
Psalm 27:6 (NKJV)

"Sing praises to God, sing praises! Sing praises to our King, sing praises!"
Psalm 47:6 (NKJV)

"While I live I will praise the Lord; I will sing praises to my God while I have my being."
Psalm 146:2 (NKJV)

TODAY'S AFFIRMATIONS

I am a true worshipper who sings praises to God from my heart.

My life is filled with songs of praise that honor God in spirit and truth.

THE WARRIOR'S MINDSET

DAY 31: He Sings Praises to The Lord

Worship is more than a religious activity—it's a heart posture that God actively seeks in His followers. True worship happens in "spirit and truth," engaging our whole being with sincere devotion based on who God truly is. Singing praises is a powerful expression of this worship, lifting our focus above our circumstances and connecting our emotions with spiritual truths. The Psalmist's repeated emphasis on singing reveals that vocal praise isn't optional but central to a life of worship. It becomes a "sacrifice of joy"—something we offer to God regardless of how we feel, and paradoxically, this very offering often transforms our feelings.

Reflection

Notice how difficult circumstances seem smaller when you're focused on God's greatness through song. If you struggle with singing or feel self-conscious, remember that God values sincerity over skill.

Action

Make singing to God part of your daily rhythm, not just at church or during designated "worship times." Choose a simple praise song or psalm and sing it throughout your day—while driving, showering, or working. You can also start by singing Scripture passages or simple phrases of gratitude.

Prayer

Father, I thank You for seeking my worship and creating me with the capacity to express praise through song. Forgive me for the times I've held back, worried about how I sound or what others might think. Help me worship You in spirit and truth, with all my heart engaged. Let praise songs rise naturally from my lips throughout each day, becoming as natural as breathing. May my singing lift my head above my circumstances and remind me of Your faithfulness. I choose to offer You sacrifices of joy through song, regardless of my situation. In Jesus' name, Amen.

Journal

_____

_____

_____

_____

_____

_____

_____

_____

_____

_____

_____

_____

_____

_____

_____

_____

_____

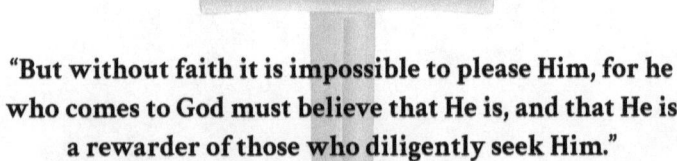

"But without faith it is impossible to please Him, for he who comes to God must believe that He is, and that He is a rewarder of those who diligently seek Him."
Hebrews 11:6 (NKJV)

TODAY'S AFFIRMATIONS

My life is fueled by faith in a God who rewards those who earnestly seek Him.

I live with confident expectation in God's goodness and faithfulness.

THE WARRIOR'S MINDSET

DAY 32: He is Fueled by Faith

Faith is not optional in the Christian life—it is essential. This verse reveals two fundamental aspects of faith: believing that God exists and believing in His character as a rewarder of those who seek Him. Faith goes beyond intellectual assent to God's existence; it involves trusting His goodness and responsiveness to our pursuit of Him. Our spiritual lives are energized and sustained by this confident expectation of God's reality and goodness. Without this faith-fuel, our spiritual engines simply cannot run in a way that pleases God.

Reflection

Identify areas in your life where you may be operating more by sight than by faith. Where do you need to trust God's character as a rewarder?

Action

Take a step of faith today by acting on God's promises rather than on what you can see or feel. This might mean forgiving someone who hasn't asked for forgiveness, giving generously when finances are tight, or praising God in the midst of difficult circumstances. Remember that diligently seeking

God always results in reward, though the reward may come in unexpected forms.

Prayer

Lord, increase my faith. Help me to live not just believing that You exist, but confidently expecting Your goodness and reward as I seek You. Forgive me for the times I've tried to operate in my own strength rather than being fueled by faith. Show me where I need to take steps of faith today, trusting Your character rather than my circumstances. I choose to diligently seek You, knowing that You are faithful to reward those who do. Let faith be the fuel that powers everything I do. In Jesus' name, Amen.

Journal

_____

_____

_____

_____

_____

_____

_____

_____

_____

_____

_____

_____

_____

_____

_____

_____

_____

_____

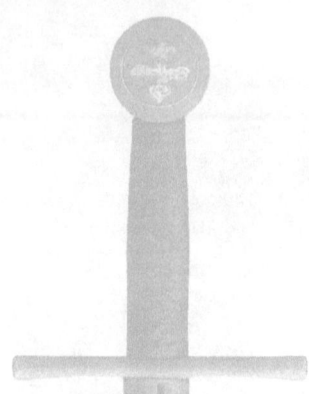

"When they had lifted up their eyes, they saw
no one but Jesus only."
Matthew 17:8 (NKJV)

"Behold, as the eyes of servants look to the hand of
their masters, as the eyes of a maid to the hand of
her mistress, so our eyes look to the LORD our
God, until He has mercy on us."
Psalm 123:2 (NKJV)

TODAY'S AFFIRMATIONS

My eyes are fixed on Jesus.

He is the lens through which I view all of life.

I see Him first and everything else through Him.

THE WARRIOR'S MINDSET

DAY 33: His Eyes are Fixed on Jesus

The spiritual warrior maintains a singular focus on Jesus Christ. Like Peter walking on water, we sink when we fix our attention on the storms and waves around us rather than on Christ. This focused gaze isn't just about admiring Jesus; it's about seeing everything else through Him. He becomes the interpretive lens through which we view our circumstances, relationships, and the world itself. This Christ-centered perspective transforms how we understand and respond to life.

Reflection

Make a conscious effort to redirect your focus whenever you notice it drifting to the waves rather than to Christ.

Action

Practice seeing your circumstances through Jesus today. When problems arise, ask, "How would Jesus see this situation?" When people frustrate you, wonder, "How does Jesus view this person?" When decisions loom, question, "What would best keep my eyes fixed on Jesus?" Make a conscious effort to redirect your focus whenever you notice it drifting to the waves rather than to Christ.

Prayer

Lord Jesus, forgive me for the many times I've fixed my eyes on my problems, other people, or my own abilities rather than on You. Help me to develop the spiritual discipline of seeing You first and seeing everything else through You. When distractions compete for my attention, draw my gaze back to You. Let me be like those disciples who, after the transfiguration experience, saw "no one but Jesus only." In Jesus' name, Amen.

Journal

_____

_____

_____

_____

_____

_____

_____

_____

_____

_____

_____

_____

_____

_____

_____

_____

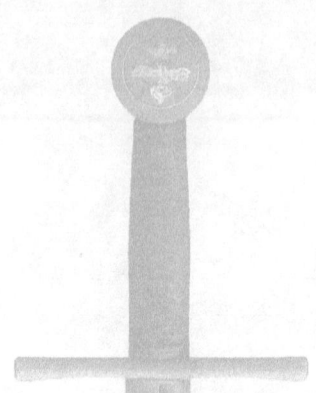

"Greater love has no one than this, than to
lay down one's life for his friends."
John 15:13 (NKJV)

TODAY'S AFFIRMATIONS

I am willing to lay down my life for Christ's kingdom.

The greatest expression of love is sacrificial, and I choose to
love as Jesus loved.

THE WARRIOR'S MINDSET

DAY 34: He Is A Living Sacrifice

Jesus defines the highest expression of love as willingness to sacrifice one's life for others. This sacrificial love stands in stark contrast to our culture's self-protective instincts. Kingdom warriors understand that genuine love requires risk and potential loss. This doesn't mean seeking martyrdom, but it does mean valuing God's kingdom and people above our own safety, comfort, and survival. When we embrace this sacrificial posture, we most closely resemble our Savior who demonstrated this love perfectly at Calvary.

Reflection

How might God be calling you to "lay down your life" today? This might not involve physical death but could mean sacrificing your time, comfort, resources, or rights for the benefit of others or the advancement of God's kingdom.

Action

Identify one specific way you can demonstrate sacrificial love today, and commit to follow through regardless of the personal cost.

Prayer

Lord Jesus, You demonstrated the greatest love by laying down Your life for me. Forgive me for clinging so tightly to my comfort, security, and rights. Give me a love that's willing to sacrifice for Your kingdom and for others. Show me specific ways I can "lay down my life" today, and grant me the courage to follow through. May my love increasingly resemble Yours—selfless, sacrificial, and kingdom-focused. In Jesus' name, Amen.

Journal

_____

_____

_____

_____

_____

_____

_____

_____

_____

_____

_____

_____

_____

_____

_____

_____

_____

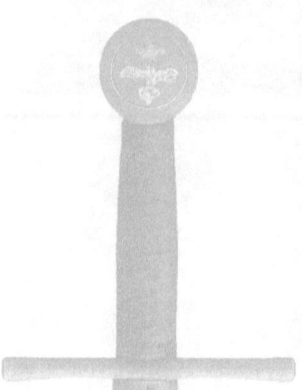

"Now thanks be to God who always leads us in triumph in Christ, and through us diffuses the fragrance of His knowledge in every place."
2 Corinthians 2:14 (NKJV)

TODAY'S AFFIRMATIONS

God always leads me in triumph in Christ.

I have been trained for victory, not defeat, and through me, the knowledge of Christ spreads and brings forth the fruit of freedom in the lives of others.

THE WARRIOR'S
MINDSET

DAY 35: He Is Trained to Triumph

God has designed the spiritual warrior for victory, not defeat. Through Christ, we are being continually led in a triumphal procession, displaying God's victory over the powers of darkness. This doesn't mean we never experience setbacks or struggles, but it does mean the ultimate trajectory of our lives is triumph, not tragedy. As we follow Christ's leadership, He ensures our participation in His victory and uses us to spread the knowledge of God everywhere, like a fragrant aroma.

Reflection

Approach today's challenges with the mindset of one who has been trained for triumph, not trained to merely survive or endure. Expect God to lead you in victory, not just occasionally but "always" as the Scripture promises.

Action

Look for opportunities to diffuse the fragrance of Christ through your attitudes, words, and actions, knowing that your triumph in Him becomes a testimony that attracts others.

Prayer

Heavenly Father, thank You for always leading me in triumph in Christ. When I'm tempted to expect defeat or to settle for mere survival, remind me that You've trained me for victory. Help me to follow Your leadership confidently, knowing the outcome is certain. Use my life to diffuse the fragrant knowledge of Christ wherever I go, drawing others to Him through the testimony of Your triumph in me. In Jesus' name, Amen.

Journal

_____

_____

_____

_____

_____

_____

_____

_____

_____

_____

_____

_____

_____

_____

_____

_____

_____

"Most assuredly, I say to you, unless a grain of
wheat falls into the ground and dies, it remains
alone; but if it dies, it produces much grain."
John 12:24 (NKJV)

TODAY'S AFFIRMATIONS

Following Christ's example, I embrace the divine principle
that my greatest fruitfulness comes through willingly dying to
self-interest, comfort, and control.

As I surrender these things in obedience, I trust His resurrection power to transform each sacrifice into a harvest that glo-
rifies Him and nourishes many.

THE WARRIOR'S MINDSET

DAY 36: He is Committed to Bearing Fruit

Jesus reveals a profound spiritual principle: fruitfulness requires death. Just as a seed must be buried and "die" before it can multiply into a harvest, we must experience a death to self before we can produce spiritual fruit. This paradoxical truth stands at the heart of Christian mission—our effectiveness for Christ's kingdom is directly proportional to our willingness to die to selfish ambition, comfort, and autonomy. The mission of Christ advances through those who, like their Master, embrace the principle of sacrificial death leading to multiplication.

Reflection

What "deaths" might God be asking of you today to increase your fruitfulness? Perhaps it's the death of a cherished plan, a comfortable routine, or a self-protective habit. Identify one area where you sense God calling you to "fall into the ground and die" so that greater fruitfulness can emerge.

Action

Take a concrete step toward embracing this necessary death, trusting the promise of multiplication that follows.

Prayer

Lord Jesus, thank You for modeling the principle of death leading to life through Your sacrifice on the cross. Help me to glorify you in my life and in my death. In Jesus' name, Amen.

Journal

_____

_____

_____

_____

_____

_____

_____

_____

_____

_____

_____

_____

_____

_____

_____

_____

_____

_____

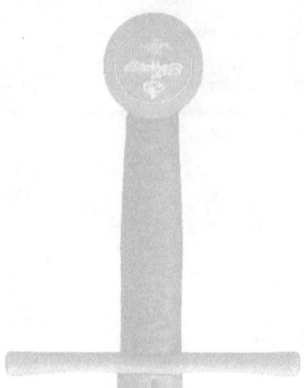

"No one can serve two masters; for either he will
hate the one and love the other, or else he will
be loyal to the one and despise the other.
You cannot serve God and mammon."
Matthew 6:24 (NKJV)

"So Jesus answered and said, 'Assuredly, I say to you,
there is no one who has left house or brothers or
sisters or father or mother or wife or children
or lands, for My sake and the gospel's...'"
Mark 10:29 (NKJV)

TODAY'S AFFIRMATIONS

I am free from the world's entanglements.

My heart is undivided, my focus clear, and my loyalty is to
Christ alone.

THE WARRIOR'S MINDSET

DAY 37: He Is Not Distracted By The World

The true warrior for Christ understands the necessity of freedom from worldly entanglements. Like a soldier who must travel light to move swiftly in battle, we too must be liberated from the cares, distractions, drama, and trauma that the world constantly presents. Jesus made it clear that divided loyalties create divided hearts. When we attempt to serve both God and the material world, we ultimately fail at both.

This freedom is not about irresponsibility or abandonment of relationships, but rather about proper prioritization. It's about recognizing that attachment to worldly things—whether possessions, status, or even unhealthy relationships—can become chains that restrict our movement in God's kingdom. The warrior knows that in releasing these attachments, true freedom is found.

Reflection

Take inventory of what occupies your mind and heart most frequently. What worldly concerns consume your thoughts, energy, and time?

Action

Identify one specific area where worldly entanglements might be holding you back from full devotion to God. Create a practical plan to begin releasing that attachment, whether through establishing boundaries, simplifying your life, or re-directing your focus to eternal matters.

Prayer

Heavenly Father, I confess that I have often tried to serve two masters. Forgive me for allowing worldly concerns to entangle my heart and distract me from Your calling. Give me the courage to re-lease those things that hinder my walk with You. Help me to find true freedom through full surrender to Your purposes. May I live as Your warrior, unencumbered by the world's cares and distractions, focused solely on advancing Your kingdom. In Jesus' name, Amen.

Journal

_____

_____

_____

_____

_____

_____

_____

_____

_____

_____

_____

_____

_____

_____

_____

_____

_____

_____

"For I consider that the sufferings of this present
time are not worthy to be compared with the
glory which shall be revealed in us."
Romans 8:18 (NKJV)

TODAY'S AFFIRMATIONS

The challenges I face today are preparing me for tomorrow's victory.

What I endure now cannot compare to the glory God will reveal in me.

THE WARRIOR'S MINDSET

DAY 38: He Accepts The Call to Suffer

Every warrior knows that rigorous training precedes glorious victory. In our spiritual journey, the challenges, hardships, and suffering we encounter are not meaningless obstacles but essential preparation for an incomparable triumph. Just as an athlete endures the pain of training with eyes fixed on the prize, we too can view our present difficulties through the lens of future glory.

Paul offers a profound perspective shift here—our current sufferings, however intense they may feel, cannot even be measured against the overwhelming weight of glory that awaits us. It's not that our struggles don't matter; rather, they matter precisely because they are producing something of such magnificent value that they pale in comparison. The challenges of training are indeed worth the inevitable victory we will experience.

Reflection

Reflect on a current difficulty you're facing. Instead of asking "Why is this happening to me?" try asking "How might God be using this to prepare me for future glory?"

Action

Write down three specific ways this challenge might be developing spiritual strength, endurance, or character in you. Then visualize the victory that lies beyond this temporary training period. How does that future perspective change your approach to today's struggle?

Prayer

Lord Jesus, thank You for the promise that my present sufferings are producing future glory. When the training feels too difficult and the challenges overwhelming, remind me that victory is certain. Give me spiritual vision to see beyond today's pain to tomorrow's triumph. Help me to embrace the challenges of training with faith and courage, knowing that You are working all things together for my good and Your glory. In Your mighty name, In Jesus' name, Amen.

Journal

_____

_____

_____

_____

_____

_____

_____

_____

_____

_____

_____

_____

_____

_____

_____

_____

_____

_____

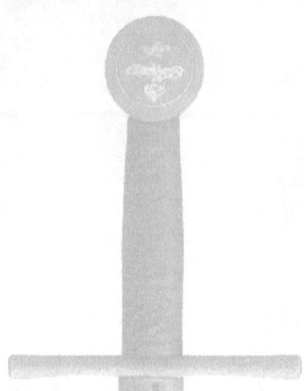

"And God will wipe away every tear from their
eyes; there shall be no more death, nor sorrow,
nor crying. There shall be no more pain, for
the former things have passed away."
Revelations 21:4 (NKJV)

TODAY'S AFFIRMATIONS

I fight knowing victory is certain.

The outcome of my battle was decided before it began—Christ
has overcome, and in Him, so have I.

THE WARRIOR'S MINDSET

DAY 39: He Knows Our Battle Has Already Been Won

A warrior who knows the outcome of the battle fights with unshakable confidence. As believers, we have been given the extraordinary privilege of knowing the end of the story—and it reveals our complete and total victory in Christ! Every tear wiped away, death itself defeated, sorrow and pain banished forever. This isn't wishful thinking but divine certainty.

Fighting with the end in mind transforms how we face today's battles. When temporary defeats, wounds, or setbacks come (and they will), they don't define us or determine our ultimate destiny. Like a soldier who presses forward despite difficult terrain, we advance with confidence, knowing that our Commander has already secured the final victory. The warrior of God fights not to win but from victory already assured.

Reflection

Identify a current struggle where you feel discouraged or defeated. Now consciously reframe it in light of God's promised victory. How does knowing the final outcome change your approach to this challenge?

Action

Make a deliberate choice today to fight not from a place of fear or uncertainty but from the unwavering confidence that victory is already yours in Christ.

Prayer

Victorious Lord, thank You for revealing the glorious end of our journey. When I am tempted to lose heart in the midst of battle, remind me that You have already declared the final outcome. Help me to fight today's battles with the confidence of certain victory. When tears come, remind me that You will one day wipe them all away. When pain persists, help me remember it is temporary. I praise You now for the victory that is already mine in Christ Jesus. In Jesus' name, Amen.

Journal

_____

_____

_____

_____

_____

_____

_____

_____

_____

_____

_____

_____

_____

_____

_____

_____

_____

"That your charitable deed may be in secret; and your Father who sees in secret will Himself reward you openly."
Matthew 6:4 (NKJV)

"Rejoice and be exceedingly glad, for great is your reward in heaven, for so they persecuted the prophets who were before you."
Matthew 5:12 (NKJV)

"Rejoice in that day and leap for joy! For indeed your reward is great in heaven, for in like manner their fathers did to the prophets."
Luke 6:23 (NKJV)

"But love your enemies, do good, and lend, hoping for nothing in return; and your reward will be great, and you will be sons of the Most High. For He is kind to the unthankful and evil."
Luke 6:35 (NKJV)

"Therefore do not cast away your confidence, which has great reward."
Hebrews 10:35 (NKJV)

v

"And behold, I am coming quickly, and My reward is with Me, to give to every one according to his work."
Revelations 22:12 (NKJV)

TODAY'S AFFIRMATIONS

I anticipate a great reward.

My Commander sees every act of obedience, and His recognition will far outweigh every sacrifice I make in His service.

THE WARRIOR'S MINDSET

DAY 40: He Anticipates His Reward From The Lord

Every warrior fights with greater intensity when a significant reward awaits victory. As spiritual warriors, we serve a generous Commander who has promised rewards beyond our imagination. These rewards are not an afterthought but a central motivation that Christ Himself offers us. He repeatedly encourages us to anticipate, rejoice in, and be motivated by the rewards He will bring.

The reward is not merely entering heaven—it is receiving specific recognition and recompense for our faithful service. The secret acts of obedience, the persecutions endured with joy, the enemies loved, the confidence maintained through trials—none of these go unnoticed or unrewarded. Our Commander keeps perfect records and promises to reward "every one according to his work." This is not salvation by works but recognition for works done through faith.

Reflection

Consider what motivates your service to God. Have you been focusing solely on duty while neglecting the joy of anticipated reward?

Action

Identify one area of obedience that feels particularly challenging right now and meditate on the specific rewards Christ promises for faithfulness in that area. Allow the anticipation of Christ's "Well done" to energize your obedience today.

Prayer

Lord Jesus, thank You for the promise of reward that awaits faithful service. When my motivation wanes or obedience becomes difficult, help me to fix my eyes on the rewards You have prepared. Thank You that You see every unseen act of service, every private sacrifice, every moment of faithfulness. Give me grace to serve with eternity's rewards in view, not seeking immediate gratification but anticipating Your "Well done." Help me to rejoice and leap for joy, knowing that my labor in You is never in vain. Come quickly, Lord Jesus, bringing Your rewards with You. In Jesus' name, Amen.

Journal

_____

_____

_____

_____

_____

_____

_____

_____

_____

_____

_____

_____

_____

_____

_____

_____

A FINAL PRAYER

Prayerfully ask God for the grace to be the warrior He's called you to be.

_____

_____

_____

_____

_____

_____

_____

_____

_____

_____

_____

_____

_____

_____

About the Author

By His Grace and for His Glory...

Patricia Daniel has served in multiple ministries over several decades, but most enjoys the Missions ministry and has served in India and Brazil. She uses her administrative gift, her English as a Second Language (ESL) certification and her writing gifts to edify the body of Christ. Patricia is the author of three other books; *In Heaven I Can Fly...A Poetic Journey of Faith*, a poetry collection, *The Purple Swan*, a children's book, and **A Block From Grace**, a memorial tribute to her parents that she co-authored.

Patricia believes we each should be living our legacy. What is legacy living? Legacy living is intentionally living your life knowing that you are here to bless others and when you influence others with your God-given gifts, your impact will outlive you. Her living legacy is *Destination Jesus,* a ministry blog where she shares her various writings, including her poetry, short stories, and bible teachings with fellow believers and those seeking Christ. Her prayer is that *Destination Jesus* would inspire others to seek God for the fulfillment of His plan for their lives and that each would live their legacy.

Why *Destination Jesus?*
Patricia's heart cry is, "It's All Him and Always Has Been and that Nothing Else Matters."

Her heart is fixed on these truths:

1. Jesus is the sole focus and end goal of our Christian faith.
2. In our surrender and service to Jesus, we find our identity, purpose, and eternal security.
3. We are destined to know Jesus, to be like Him, and to share Him with others.
4. In Jesus, we find fulfillment and can live a legacy of faith.

For more inspiration from this author, visit
Destination-Jesus.com